What Can I See on the Island?

By Yvette-Maree Van Schaemelhout

Illustrated by Alysha Blackley

Library For All Ltd.

Dugong

Dingy

Fish

8

Crocodile

Island

Turtle

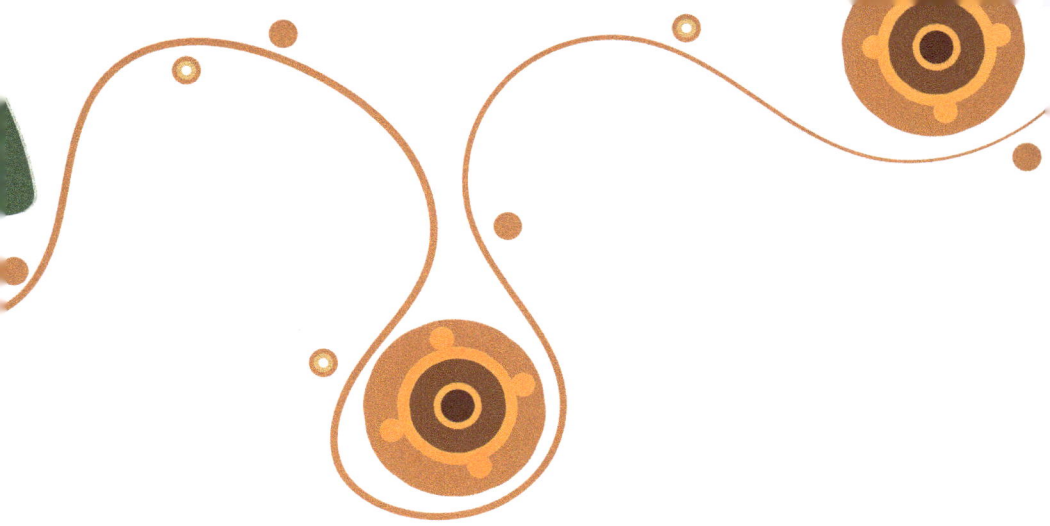

Mango

Shell

Reef

Oyster

Coconut

You can use these questions to talk about this book with your family, friends and teachers.

What did you learn from this book?

Describe this book in one word. Funny? Scary? Colourful? Interesting?

How did this book make you feel when you finished reading it?

What was your favourite part of this book?

Download the Library For All Reader app from libraryforall.org

About the contributors

Yvette-Maree Van Schaemelhout was born and raised in South Brisbane, but through her mother she is connected to Mer Island in the Torres Strait. She loves to share a meal and talk with her family. As a child she loved the story *Dot and the Kangaroo*.

Alysha was born in Mt Isa, Queensland, on the land of the Kalkutungu (Kalkadoon) people. She is of both Aboriginal and Torres Strait Islander descent, with connections to Kalkutungu and Moa Island, Kubin Village.
Alysha is a young artist who began her artistic journey through graphic design, and now completes freelance artworks for many First Nations peoples. She finds true pride in helping and supporting her people by bringing their ideas to life.

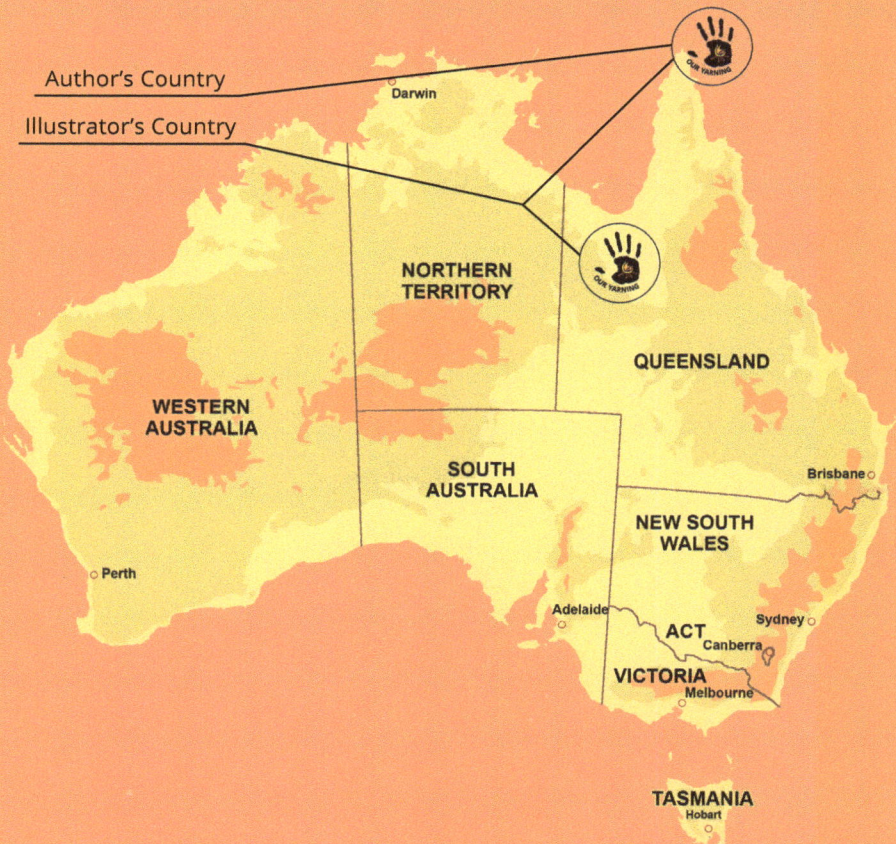

Author's Country

Illustrator's Country

Darwin

NORTHERN
TERRITORY

QUEENSLAND

WESTERN
AUSTRALIA

SOUTH
AUSTRALIA

Brisbane

NEW SOUTH
WALES

Perth

Adelaide

Sydney

ACT
Canberra

VICTORIA

Melbourne

TASMANIA
Hobart

Our Yarning

The Our Yarning collection aligns with the Australian Curriculum through the Cross-Curriculum Priorities — Aboriginal and Torres Strait Islander Histories and Cultures. The collection provides an authentic opportunity for learning and embedding Aboriginal and Torres Strait Islander perspectives because it is written by Aboriginal and Torres Strait Islander people.

We know that children learn better, and enjoy reading more, when they see themselves in the stories, characters and illustrations of the books they read.

To download the app, visit the Google Play Store or Apple Store and search 'Our Yarning'.

libraryforall.org

You're reading Learner

Learner – Beginner readers

Start your reading journey with short words, big ideas and plenty of pictures.

Level 1 – Rising readers

Raise your reading level with more words, simple sentences and exciting images.

Level 2 – Eager readers

Enjoy your reading time with familiar words, but complex sentences.

Level 3 – Progressing readers

Develop your reading skills with creative stories and some challenging vocabulary.

Level 4 – Fluent readers

Step up your reading skills with playful narratives, new words and fun facts.

Middle Primary – Curious readers

Discover your world through science and stories.

Upper Primary – Adventurous readers

Explore your world through science and stories.

www.ingramcontent.com/pod-product-compliance
Lightning Source LLC
Chambersburg PA
CBHW042342040426
42448CB00019B/3379